the

PURSUIT

of

HOLINESS

JERRY BRIDGES

STUDY GUIDE

NAVPRESS

NAVPRESS⊘.

NavPress is the publishing ministry of The Navigators, an international Christian organization and leader in personal spiritual development. NavPress is committed to helping people grow spiritually and enjoy lives of meaning and hope through personal and group resources that are biblically rooted, culturally relevant, and highly practical.

For a free catalog go to www.NavPress.com
or call 1.800.366.7788 in the United States or 1.800.839.4769 in Canada.

ISBN 978-1-57683-988-1

Cover design by www.studiogearbox.com
Cover photo by Getty/Michael Cogliantry
Interior design by www.pamelapoll.com

Printed in the United States of America

4 5 6 7 / 11 10 09

Contents

Before You Begin

What is holiness? Do I fully understand my responsibility for living a holy life? Why do I experience defeat in the struggle against sin? What has God provided to help me overcome sin?

To help you in a personal discovery of God's principles for holy living, this Bible study course serves as a companion to the book *The Pursuit of Holiness*. Its objective is to guide you into direct study of many Scripture passages on which the book is based.

The course consists of twelve lessons, which encompass all seventeen chapters in *The Pursuit of Holiness*. For each, you will read a chapter or chapters from the book, look up Scripture passages and answer questions about the lesson's topic. Then you will plan a way to apply the truths of the lesson to your life. Within each lesson is an optional question for further study of the Scriptures.

Before beginning each lesson, ask God to clarify the Scriptures to you and to reveal Himself in new ways as you study His Word.

Use a pen or pencil to underline or mark key statements as you read the book, and have this Bible study booklet opened to the lesson. During your reading, jot down in the appropriate space any observations about the text you want to remember, as well as other Scripture passages or incidents from your life or the lives of others that illustrate the truths of the chapter, and any questions that come to your mind. This section can be one of the most profitable for you in each lesson, allowing you to expand upon the material presented in the text.

As you study the Scripture passages in the lesson and answer the questions, and as you prepare to write an application at the end, ask yourself these questions:

◆ What do these passages teach about God's will for a holy life?
◆ How does my life measure up to Scripture? Where and how do I fall short?
◆ What definite steps of action do I need to take to obey God?

Write down not only the scriptural truth you want to apply, but also a practical, specific statement and plan for making the application.

The most profitable way of doing this study is to do it yourself first, then meet with a group of others who are doing it also. Discuss your discoveries, questions, and applications in the group.

As you learn more about our calling from "the high and exalted One, who lives forever, whose name is Holy" (Isaiah 57:15), may you experience new commitment and joy in holy living.

Holiness Is for You

1. Read chapters 1 and 2 of *The Pursuit of Holiness*. Record below the major observations, illustrations, or questions that come to your mind as you read the chapters.

2. Look again at the three reasons why we do not experience more personal holiness (pages 16-18). Which of them applies most to your life? Can you think of other reasons?

3. Look up the following verses and meditate on what each one says about God's holiness. Copy from your Bible the verse or verses which are the most meaningful to you, and explain why they are.

Exodus 15:11; Leviticus 19:1-2; Psalm 89:35; Isaiah 57:15; I Peter 1:14-16

4. Write a sentence for each of the following verses telling what it teaches about God's holiness.

Habakkuk 1:13 – *God can't even look at holiness*

Zechariah 8:17 – *God hates when we even imagine evil*

James 1:13 – *God can't tempt us w/ evil*

5. (*For additional study*) Look up the following verses, analyzing what each one teaches about God's holiness or holiness in the Christian. Copy from your Bible the passages which are most helpful to you, and explain why they are.

1 Samuel 13:13-14; Psalm 51:4; Isaiah 6:1-5; 40:25; Jeremiah 51:5; Ezekiel 39:7; Romans 6:14; 1 John 1:5; Revelation 4:8; 22:11

6. In your own words write a definition of holiness.

7. What application of the truths of this lesson do you want to make in your life?

Holiness Is Not an Option

1. Read chapter 3 of *The Pursuit of Holiness*. Record below the major observations, illustrations, or questions that come to your mind as you read the chapter.

2. What do the following verses teach about our holy *standing* before God? (Note: The word *sanctified*, used in some Bible versions, means "made holy.")

Romans 5:19

Hebrews 10:10

✗ 1 Peter 3:18

3. What do the following verses teach about holy *living*?

Ephesians 4:1,30

1 Thessalonians 4:7

Titus 2:11-12 – *what does soberly ~~righteously~~ mean?*

4. Look up the verses below. From each one write a brief statement on why holiness is not optional for a Christian.

Psalm 66:18

Romans 8:13-14

2 Timothy 2:21

1 John 1:6

5. Consider Hebrews 12:14. What further efforts do you need to make toward holiness in your life?

6. *(For additional study)* Look up the following verses, analyzing what each one teaches about our holy standing before God and the need for holy living. Copy from your Bible the passages which are the most helpful to you, and explain why they are.

Psalms 15:1-5; 32:3-4; Isaiah 64:6-7; Matthew 1:21; 7:21-23; 1 Corinthians 1:2; 2 Corinthians 5:17; Ephesians 1:4; James 2:14-26; 1 John 3:2-5

7. What application of the truths of this lesson do you want to make in your life?

The Holiness of Christ

1. Read chapter 4 of *The Pursuit of Holiness*. Write down the major observations, illustrations, or questions you have from reading the chapter.

2. After studying the following verses, write a statement of what the holiness of Christ means to you in your personal pursuit of holiness.

Isaiah 6:5-7; Ephesians 5:1-2; 1 Timothy 1:15; 1 Peter 2:21

3. Look up the following verses about the holiness of Jesus Christ. Copy from your Bible those which are the most meaningful to you, and explain why they are.

Isaiah 53:11; John 8:29; 2 Corinthians 5:21; Hebrews 1:9; 4:15; 1 Peter 2:22; 1 John 3:5

4. If Satan questions your salvation with the thought, "A true Christian wouldn't think the evil thoughts you've been thinking today," how should you respond?

5. *(For additional study)* Look up the following verses about the holiness of Christ. Which are the most significant to you? Why?

John 4:34; 6:38; 8:45-49; Hebrews 10:7; 1 Peter 1:18-19

6. What application of the truths of this lesson do you want to make in your life?

The Battle for Holiness

1. Read chapters 5 and 6 of *The Pursuit of Holiness*. Record the major observations, illustrations, or questions you have from your reading.

2. Study Romans 6:1-12 and Colossians 1:13. In your own words, what does it mean to have died to sin?

3. What does each of the following verses teach about our hearts and sin?

Jeremiah 17:9-10

Mark 7:21-23

Romans 7:18

4. Using the following verses, explain the nature of our desires and why we need to watch them closely.

Ephesians 4:20-22; Titus 3:3; James 1:14-15

5. (*For additional study*) Look up the following verses about our struggle against sin, write down those which are the most helpful to you, and explain why they are.

Genesis 6:5-6; Psalm 139:23-24; Proverbs 4:23; Luke 6:45; Acts 26:18; Romans 6:17-23; 1 Corinthians 10:12; Galatians 5:17; 6:1; Hebrews 4:12; James 1:22; 1 John 3:9

6. Why, if we died to sin, do we still sin?

7. As those who have died to sin, what is our responsibility with regard to sin now?

8. What application of the truths of this lesson do you want to make in your own life?

God's Provision and Our Responsibility

1. Read chapters 7 and 8 of *The Pursuit of Holiness*. Write down the major observations, illustrations, or questions you have from your reading.

2. Carefully consider Romans 6:11. What does this verse mean to you, and how can you apply it to your life?

3. Review Isaiah 66:2 and 1 Thessalonians 5:23-24. How should we express our dependence on the Holy Spirit for holiness? What do you want to do to improve in this area?

4. From each of the following verses, write a brief statement of how the Holy Spirit helps us in our pursuit of holiness.

Romans 8:9

Romans 8:13

Galatians 5:16

Ephesians 3:16

Philippians 2:12-13

5. Read the following verses, and write a statement describing your personal responsibility for holiness.

Hebrews 12:1; James 4:7; 2 Peter 3:14

6. *(For additional study)* Look up the following verses about the Holy Spirit's work in us, write down those which are the most helpful to you, and explain why they are.

    I Corinthians 6:18-19; Ephesians 3:14-21; Philippians 4:11-13; Colossians 1:9-11; I Thessalonians 4:7-8

7. How can we express at the same time both an attitude of dependence on the Holy Spirit and acceptance of our own responsibility for holiness?

8. What application of the truths of this lesson do you want to make in your life?

Putting Sin to Death

1. Read chapter 9 of *The Pursuit of Holiness*. Write down the major observations, illustrations, or questions you have from your reading.

2. After considering Romans 8:13 and Colossians 3:5, write in your own words what it means to "put to death" the sinful deeds in our lives.

3. How do the following verses help us develop personal convictions about issues that are not specifically mentioned in the Bible?

1 Corinthians 6:12-13

1 Corinthians 8:4-13

1 Corinthians 10:23-33

4. Read through Romans 14, and list the principles that can help us in areas in which Christians have different convictions.

5. What do the following verses teach about the importance of commitment to holiness?

Proverbs 27:20

Luke 14:33

1 John 2:1

6. *(For additional study)* Consider what these verses teach about commitment, conviction, and obedience. Write down those which are the most helpful to you, and explain why they are.

   Deuteronomy 17:18-20; Psalm 119:9-11; John 14:21; Romans 12:1-2

7. Using at least one Scripture passage to document your answer, explain how we develop conviction about the necessity of living a holy life and about obedience to God in specific areas of our lives.

8. How do you think Scripture memory can help in developing conviction?

9. What application of the truths of this lesson do you want to make in your life?

The Place of Personal Discipline

1. Read chapter 10 of *The Pursuit of Holiness*. Write down the major observations, illustrations, or questions you have from your reading.

2. What does each of the following passages teach about Christian discipline?

   1 Corinthians 9:24-27

1 Timothy 4:7-8

2 Timothy 3:16

3. Look up the following verses. Why is perseverance needed in Christian discipline? How can these verses help us to persevere?

Proverbs 24:16; 1 Corinthians 15:58; Hebrews 12:3

4. *(For additional study)* Examine how each of these verses relates to discipline in the Christian life. Write down those which are the most helpful to you, and explain why they are.

Joshua 1:8-9; Romans 7:15; Ephesians 4:20-24; Hebrews 12:1-2; James 1:22-25

5. What does it mean to meditate on Scripture? Suggest a plan for meditation that would be suitable for you and your schedule.

6. In your own words, write a definition of discipline.

7. What application of the truths of this lesson do you want to make in your life?

Holiness in Body

1. Read chapter 11 of *The Pursuit of Holiness*. Write down the major observations, illustrations, or questions you have from your reading.

2. The following three verses give practical ways to resist temptation. In what areas of your life can these verses help you?

Proverbs 27:12

Romans 13:14

2 Timothy 2:22

3. *(For additional study)* Examine how each of these verses relates to bodily holiness. Write down those which are the most helpful to you, and explain why they are.

Philippians 3:17-19; Colossians 3:5-7; 1 Timothy 6:17; Hebrews 13:5; 1 John 2:15-16

4. After reading the following verses, write a statement about the importance of holiness in body.

Romans 6:12-13; 12:1-2; 1 Corinthians 6:19-20; 9:27

5. Why is it important for the Christian to govern his indulgence of food and drink?

6. In what ways does materialism affect our holiness of body?

7. What application of the truths of this lesson do you want to make in your life?

Holiness in Spirit

1. Read chapter 12 of *The Pursuit of Holiness*. Write down the major observations, illustrations, or questions you have from your reading.

2. From each of the following verses, write a statement about the importance of holiness in our thoughts.

   1 Samuel 16:7

Psalm 139:1-4

2 Corinthians 7:1

3. Compare your own thought life with the standard set for us in Philippians 4:8. What types of thoughts do you need to avoid? What types of thoughts do you want to cultivate?

4. How we think is affected by what we see and hear. From the following verses, explain the Bible's standards in these two areas.

Matthew 5:27-28; Ephesians 5:3-4; 1 Timothy 2:9-10

5. Study Galatians 5:19-21. Which of these acts of the sinful nature listed in the passage are most apt to be present in Christians? Which do you think are the most dangerous to you in your life?

6. Describe the unholy thinking referred to in each of the following passages.

1 Samuel 18:6-12

Psalm 73:12-14,21

Matthew 18:21-35

Luke 15:22-32

Luke 18:9-14

7. *(For additional study)* Examine how each of the following verses relates to holiness in spirit, write down those which are the most helpful to you, and explain why they are.

Genesis 37:3-11; Job 31:1; Proverbs 1:10-16; Matthew 5:21-22; Romans 12:19; 1 Peter 2:21-23; 4:3-5

8. What application of the truths of this lesson do you want to make in your life?

Holiness and Our Wills

1. Read chapters 13 and 14 of *The Pursuit of Holiness*. Write down the major observations, illustrations, or questions you have from your reading.

2. How do the following verses describe our responsibility concerning our reason, emotions, and will?

   Romans 6:19

Romans 12:2

Colossians 3:1-2

James 4:7-8

3. Carefully read Proverbs 2:1-12. If we desire to guard our minds from evil, what must we do?

4. List at least two "success" stories from the Bible (see page 128-129 in *The Pursuit of Holiness*) that especially appeal to you and which you can continually refer to for motivation to holiness.

5. *(For additional study)* Examine how each of these verses relates to holiness and our wills, emotions, or reason. Write down those which are the most meaningful to you, and explain why they are.

   Genesis 3:1-6; Psalm 1:1-2; John 5:39-40; Ephesians 4:17-19; Philippians 2:12-13; 2 Timothy 2:22

6. Explain in your own words how the reason, emotions, and will are related, and how they work together.

7. Review the four principles for acquiring or breaking a habit listed in chapter 14. Select a habit you want to acquire or break, and write how each of the four principles can help you.

8. What other application of the truths in this lesson do you want to make in your life?

Holiness and Faith

1. Read chapter 15 of *The Pursuit of Holiness*. Write down the major observations, illustrations, or questions you have from your reading.

2. Explain the relationship you see between faith and obedience in Hebrews 3:17-19 and 4:2,6.

3. Read through Hebrews 11, noting the instances of obedience by faith. List five things which some of the persons mentioned in this chapter believed. Which is the most meaningful for you, and why?

4. List five ways in which the persons mentioned in Hebrews 11 obeyed God. Which is the most challenging example for you, and why?

5. *(For additional study)* Review the principles given in the following verses. Explain how faith is required to follow each one, and under what circumstances the principle would be the most difficult for you to believe.

Matthew 20:26-27; Luke 6:30-31; Romans 12:19; 1 Timothy 6:17-18; Hebrews 3:13

6. In *The Pursuit of Holiness* we have seen holiness defined as the state of being "morally blameless" (page 15), "conformity to the moral precepts of the Bible" (page 15), "conformity to the character of God" (page 22), and "obedience to the will of God in whatever God directs" (page 136). From what you have learned in this and the previous lessons, write a summary definition of holiness which is meaningful to you, then compare it with the definition you wrote in lesson 1, question 6.

7. What application of the truths in this lesson do you want to make in your life?

Holiness in
an Unholy World

1. Read chapters 16 and 17 of *The Pursuit of Holiness*. Write down the major observations, illustrations, or questions you have from your reading.

2. After studying the following verses, summarize what they teach about the Christian's relationship to an unholy world.

Matthew 5:13-14; John 17:14-16; 1 Peter 3:15-16

3. From the following verses, explain what the Christian's response should be when he is ridiculed or abused for his holy life.

Matthew 5:11-12; John 15:19; 2 Timothy 3:12; 1 Peter 2:12; 4:12-13

4. How can we follow the example of Jesus in associating with unholy people (read Luke 5:29-32) and at the same time keep ourselves holy as He did (Hebrews 7:26)? List some actual situations you might face in which this would be difficult.

5. Read 1 Corinthians 10:13. How can this promise help you in some unholy environment you may be in?

6. *(For additional study)* Examine how each of the following verses relates to holiness in an unholy world, or to the joy of holiness. Write down those which are the most helpful to you, and explain why they are.

Psalm 51:10-12; I Corinthians 5:9-10; Ephesians 5:5-12; Philippians 2:14-15; I Peter 4:3-4; 2 Peter 2:7-9; Hebrews 12:1-2

7. What does each of the following verses teach about the joy of a holy life?

Nehemiah 8:9-10

Psalm 16:11

John 15:10-11

Romans 14:17

8. What application of the truths in this lesson do you want to make in your life?

Author

Jerry Bridges is a staff member of The Navigators Collegiate Ministries where he is involved in staff training and also serves as a resource person to those ministering on university campuses.

He has been on staff of the Navigators since 1955. From 1979 through 1994, he served as Vice President for Corporate Affairs. In addition to his work in the Collegiate Ministries, he also serves from time to time as a guest lecturer at several seminaries and speaks at numerous conferences and retreats, both in the U.S. and overseas. In 2005, Jerry received an honorary doctorate from Westminster Theological Seminary.

The Pursuit of Holiness, which has sold more than a million copies. Other titles in print are: *The Practice of Godliness, Trusting God, Transforming Grace, The Discipline of Grace, The Gospel for Real Life, Is God Really in Control?, The Crisis of Caring,* and *The Joy of Fearing God.* Jerry and his wife, Jane, live in Colorado Springs, Colorado. They have two adult children and five grandchildren.

CLASSICS FROM JERRY BRIDGES.

Is God Really in Control?

978-1-57683-931-7
Now you can learn to trust God's wisdom, love, and sovereignty in the midst of life's minor disappointments and major tragedies. Experience comfort and hope by exploring the greater purposes of God.

Trusting God

978-1-60006-305-3
It's easy to trust God when everything's going your way. But what about when things go wrong? Learn the essentials of belief necessary to trust God completely.

Transforming Grace

978-1-60006-303-9
The transforming grace to help you accept and understand God's grace so you can live with the freedom of not having to measure up.

The Practice of Godliness

978-089109-941-3
It's easy to get caught up in doing things for God rather than being *with* God. Learn how to be godly in the midst of life by being committed to God instead of activities.

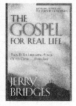

The Gospel for Real Life

978-1-57683-507-4
Find out how the gospel is more than eternal salvation, setting you free daily from sin's defeat and empowering you to experience God's abundant life. Now includes a study guide.

To order copies, call NavPress at 1-800-366-7788
or log on to www.navpress.com.